I BELIEVE
IN GOD

I BELIEVE
IN GOD

Costen J. Harrell

ABINGDON PRESS
New York • *Nashville*

I BELIEVE IN GOD

Copyright © MCMLVIII by Abingdon Press

Library of Congress Catalog Card Number: 58-5397

SET UP, PRINTED, AND BOUND BY THE
PARTHENON PRESS, AT NASHVILLE,
TENNESSEE, UNITED STATES OF AMERICA

CONTENTS

CHAPTER I

THE REALITY OF GOD

RUDYARD KIPLING WAS ONCE VERY ILL IN A NEW YORK hotel. The nurse attending him bent over and asked if he wanted anything. "Yes," he replied, "I want my heavenly Father."

What Kipling said in an hour of desperation is the language of man in every age and place. Belief in God is not a spiritual luxury in which one may indulge himself, but stark necessity to an ordered and satisfying life. Long ago a psalmist sang, "Lord, thou hast been our dwelling place in all generations." In God, as around our hearthstone, we find security and happiness. One sentence from Augustine is more frequently quoted than any other: "Thou hast made us for thyself and restless is our heart until it comes to rest in thee." We may misunderstand him; we may ignore him; we may openly deny him, but there is in every breast a yearning, "uttered or unexpressed," for the knowledge of the living God. If, perchance, above the noise and strife of things, any man has a strong, sure word to speak concerning God, he will not lack for an audience.

The fundamental idea of Christianity is the fact of

God. This is not a modern idea, conceived in our times and therefore likely to have its day and cease to be, as many ideas do. It is rooted in the long past. It has come to flower in the Christian faith. It has been challenged by intellectuals, so-called; it has been denied by men who were bent on having their own way; it has been ridiculed by scorners. And yet there are more persons on the earth today that believe in God as he is revealed and interpreted in the Christian faith than ever before in the history of mankind. Persuaded that the insights of the Bible are true, supported by the testimony of the best and most intelligent men and women of every age, assured by their daily experience of him, unnumbered millions of every nation and race stand on their feet every Lord's Day and shout in the face of the world, "I believe in God the Father Almighty, Maker of heaven and earth." This is the first affirmation of the Christian's creed. It is Christianity's rallying call to all the races of men. Unless we are sure of God we can be sure of nothing, and all our religious beliefs and sentiments crumble like a house built on drifting sand.

Is our belief in God justifiable? Is the fact of God so established as to assure both mind and heart? Is it trustworthy enough to live by—and to die by? These pages are written in the sure conviction that the fact of God is undeniable, and in the hope that they may in some measure make plain the reason for the faith that is in us.

These pages are also a personal confession, the fruit of the author's increasing experience and assurance of

"God the Father Almighty." Who could be more real in an ordered world like this than he who is the architect and builder of it? He is evident everywhere—in nature's simple beauty and in her majestic grandeur—in man's ceaseless struggle to find a better way—in the faces of those who believe and love and serve—and in the secret places of our own souls where a Voice is heard with unmistakable clarity. And sometimes rare moments come when a sense of his presence sweeps over the spirit, like breezes from the highlands, and the heart breaks forth in singing, "Bless the Lord, O my soul, and all that is within me, bless his holy name!"

Belief in God is inescapable

"I believe in God"—this is a momentous declaration. No confession that an intelligent being may make is so fundamental, or so far-reaching in its implications.

It has sometimes been said with an air of smart finality that what one believes does not matter so long as he lives an upright and useful life. The assumption is utterly false. We cannot escape the fundamentals. A very wise man once remarked, "There is nothing so practical as a fundamental"—that is, what we genuinely believe to be true and final determines our practical, everyday living and in the end molds our character. Of every man it may be said, "As he thinketh in his heart, so is he." What we believe determines how we live. And no belief so sets the course of our living as what we think of God and our relation to him.

9

Suppose one assumes that God is not!—though this is for me an impossible assumption! But, suppose one persuaded himself that God is only a kind of celestial Santa Claus, fashioned out of man's imagination, a mythical figure which we have devised because of our childishness. Think how disastrous such a belief would be to all our thinking and living. We would be as pilgrims at midnight with no light to walk by.

Should one deny that there is an infinite Intelligence behind all that is, then he has no recourse except to believe that everything that is has come to be by sheer chance. One must believe in blind chance or in an intelligent God. There is no other alternative. And, if he should declare his belief that all things come by chance or accident, then he must admit that there can be no ultimate plan or purpose in anything that is. That is to say, that all the wonder and order of creation came by accident out of chaos, and by the same process are drifting back to chaos. And since man is a part of creation—the crown and glory of it, as the Bible teaches—he must suffer the same fate. I could no more believe that this marvelous universe, including man and all his powers to think and to achieve, could come into being by chance than I could believe that a cat, running up and down the keyboard of a piano, could in a hundred million years produce "The Star-Spangled Banner" or Schubert's "Serenade"!

When an atheist's denial of God is translated into daily living, the results are disastrous beyond all words to describe. If God is banished from one's thoughts, there is for him no ultimate standard of moral right. Good and evil have no meaning except to serve our immediate needs and convenience. The sacrifices of a martyr and the crimes of gangsters are only different ways for arriving—*nowhere.* The best that a God-less interpretation of life has to offer is a brief moment of conscious existence—a little ride on the merry-go-round and in the end to get off where we started.

> One moment in Annihilation's Waste,
> One moment, of the Well of Life to taste—
> The Stars are setting and the Caravan
> Starts for the Dawn of Nothing. . . .

Why should one who does not believe in God strive to live righteously? Why should he respect honor and truth? Virtues have no worth and love no meaning apart from God. Truth and right are rooted in his being and character. We hold that conduct that is god-like is good, and that sin in the end leads to disaster because it is contrary to the nature and purpose of God. To attempt to uphold moral standards without belief in God is like attempting to carry water in a bucket without a bottom. Wickedness and despair are the offspring of unbelief. Our beliefs inevitably work themselves out in our living. Atheistic communism denied the existence of God, and then followed, as the night the day, the denial of all moral law.

But there is a more excellent way. Suppose it is true

that "behind the dim unknown, standeth God." Suppose that the whole creation is the work of his infinite goodness and wisdom. And suppose he controls all things in harmony with his high and holy purpose. And more—suppose we are assured that the power that holds the stars in their courses cares for us, and suppose we are persuaded that God is calling each of us to become like him and in kinship of soul to have fellowship with him forever. Does not such a belief concerning God change our whole attitude toward life, and stir us to noble endeavor?

These are not mere suppositions, but solid truths. They are the Christian's creed. I believe them with mind and heart and intuition. In their strong clear light creation and history and religion make sense. Supported by such a faith as this, hope springs eternal in the breast. We dare to live and undertake, and in the face of every disaster cry, "We are more than conquerors through him that loved us."

I am not inclined to argue concerning God. Rather, I look out upon the world and into my heart and say, God is inescapable.

God is a Person

When we affirm that God plans and acts, that he is righteous and cares for us mortals, we thereby affirm that he is a Person. An impersonal force cannot do these things. Electricity is a force, but it has no consciousness of its strange power and no ability to direct it to serve a desired end. Only an intelligent mind can use it to light an incandescent bulb. Intelligence, decision, freedom of action, righteousness, love—all these are personal qualities. Because the Creator and Governor of the universe possesses them he is a Person. If we believe in God, intelligent and active, we cannot escape the conviction that he is a Person. If we believe less, we make him inferior to man, and no God at all!

At the center of all things is a Mind and Heart like our own. The experiences of life, the knowledge and insights which we gain through the fleeting years—all these compel us to alter and enlarge our childhood's idea of the Almighty, but we can never outgrow the fundamental truth that he thinks and wills and loves and acts. This is only another way of saying that God is a Person.

Some years ago a young medical student came to my study and said with manifest feeling, "This week, I found God in the dissecting room." In the mechanism of the human body, so "fearfully and wonderfully made," he had discovered unmistakable proof of a Mind wonderful beyond compare. Every man knows that intelligence is required to understand, even dimly, this mysterious universe, whether the movements of the stars or the secrets of an atom, or the body of a man. To imagine for an instant that intelligence is required to understand what intelligence did not create, is to abandon reason and common sense.

Infinite intelligence appears in all creation, and we

think God's thoughts after him. A Voice speaks to our conscience, and we cannot deny its authority. Infinite love calls us, and we respond. "Deep calleth unto deep," and we commune with God as friend with friend. Religion is a personal relationship between finite man and the infinite God, and anything less than that is unworthy of the name. It is the fellowship of person with Person—of man with God.

God is a mystery

Our limited minds cannot fully comprehend God. The infinite will always be beyond the reach of us finite mortals. Concerning God there are questions that none can answer. Enveloping him are mysteries that no one can penetrate. This has been the common experience of the best and wisest men in their search after the Father Almighty. In the book of Job a discerning man recognizes the limitations of man's knowledge: "Canst thou by searching find out God? Canst thou find out the Almighty unto perfection?"

The revelation of God in Jesus Christ does not remove the mystery. Rather, the wonder grows. Living in the early afterglow of Jesus' years on the earth, Paul exclaimed: "O the depth of the riches both of the wisdom and knowledge of God! how unsearchable are his judgments, and his ways past finding out! For who hath known the mind of the Lord?"

14

We cannot evade the mysteries. In every phase of our living we are engulfed by them. No one can explain how out of black soil a green stem appears, and out of the stem a violet whose loveliness and fragrance awaken in us a strange, sweet joy. We do not solve the mystery by describing the process of its growth, or by naming what we cannot understand. In a single violet there is a mystery of life that no one has fathomed. And if a tiny flower holds a mystery too great for our minds, how much more the everlasting God!

If we could dissolve the mystery of God and answer all questions that might be asked concerning him, we would be as wise as he. We pray to him because his wisdom and power are infinitely greater than ours. We worship him because he transcends all that we are able to think. Religion does not answer all our questions. Rather, it awakens in us the sense and surety of a Presence, real and yet veiled in mystery, near and yet transcendent— and sets the heart to singing: "Holy, holy, holy, Lord God of hosts, heaven and earth are full of thy glory."

While we cannot know *everything* about God, we do know *something*. A bucket cannot contain the ocean, but it may be filled out of the ocean's abundance. We cannot explain the mystery of God, but we may, nevertheless, know him. We may experience him as a living reality, and, sustained by a sense of his presence, live our years victoriously and greet the unknown with a cheer. The order of things around us, the long experience of the race, God's revelation of himself, and the witness of our own hearts give substance to our faith.

We attempt to lift up some plain and simple things that support and confirm our belief in the reality of God.

CHAPTER II

GOD IN NATURE

NATURE IS GOD'S OPEN BOOK. THE BIBLE, THOUGH containing I firmly believe a divine message, was written by human hands. This treasury of truth is both human and divine. But "no human creature has ever been permitted to collaborate with the Eternal in the unfolding of the morning or in the painting of a dying day—in the decking of the springtime or in the creation of the pageantry of a cloudless night. There are no human fingerprints either on the ocean or on the clouds." On the fiftieth birthday of Agassiz, the great naturalist, Longfellow wrote his friend some lines in which he describes nature as speaking to this man who loved her ways and her mysteries—

> "Come, wander with me," she said,
> "Into regions yet untrod;
> And read what is still unread
> In the manuscripts of God."

These "manuscripts of God" are not hidden in libraries. They are not the especial possession of the learned and the privileged. They are open to all men everywhere. "There is no speech nor language, where their voice is not heard. Their line is gone out through all the earth, and their words to the end of the world."

And what an incomparable story they tell? We owe an immeasurable debt to modern scientists, for by patient toil they have revealed to us God's methods. They have uncovered secrets and wonders we would not have dreamed of. There is no conflict between genuine science and true religion. Irreligious science and unreasonable religion are in continual disagreement. Our minds and tempers are steadied when we remember that all truth is God's truth, and that he does not contradict himself. The Lord of nature is also Lord of our souls.

One's belief in God should never be disturbed by any scientific discovery. No scientist can change nature's laws one jot or tittle. He only reports them. When science reports some new wonder—the splitting of an atom or the discovery of another constellation in the sky—we marvel anew at the unlimited resources of the Creator. Scientists have been our teachers in religion as well as in chemistry and physics. They have opened the windows of our minds to the greatness and goodness of God. The more we learn of his magnificence, the more our hearts are moved to worship him. The words of a psalmist should have deeper meaning for a student in a modern laboratory than for the man who wrote them: "Marvellous are thy works; and that my soul knoweth right well." If nature were my only teacher, I think I could not escape belief in a divine Intelligence and in a sovereign God.

Order in the vastness

The splendor of a midnight sky turns our thoughts to awe and wonder. And who can gaze upon the stars without reflecting that—

> The spangled heavens, a shining frame,
> Their great Original proclaim?

What the astronomers are telling us about the vastness of this created order is like a hymn of praise to the magnificence of the Creator.

On the first page of his remarkable book *The Mysterious Universe,* Sir James Jeans, one of the world's foremost astronomers, writes words that amaze us:

The total number of stars in the universe is probably something like the total number of grains of sand on all the seashores of the world. . . . This vast multitude of stars are wandering about in space. . . . They travel through a universe so spacious that it is an event of almost unimaginable rarity for a star to come anywhere near to another star. For the most part each voyages in splendid isolation, like a ship on an empty ocean.

When we read of such a universe, we can only exclaim in the words of a psalmist: "Such knowledge is too wonderful for me; it is high, I cannot attain unto it."

The giant 200-inch telescope at Mount Palomar Observatory in California reveals the location of stars so far distant from the earth that it requires a billion years for their light to reach us. When we measure this by the amazing speed of light, we begin to conceive something of the utter vastness of creation. Such spaces are beyond our mental grasp. They are beyond the limits of our imagination. Indeed, we are citizens of no mean universe!

A greater wonder awaits us. Every portion of this vast universe is under control. The searchers of the sky find that everywhere there is evidence of the work of a Mind like our minds. The stars keep their appointed courses. It explains nothing to say that they do this by the law of the attraction of bodies. How did such laws come into being? Natural law is only a method by which intelligence works. Our nights are not made fearful by the collision of heavenly bodies. The rotation of the earth on its axis is so accurately determined that it does not vary one second in a century.

The earth and the sky combine to teach us how magnificent and how dependable God is. If we can trust him in the vast movements of the sky—as we must—can we not trust him in the smaller orbits of our living?

Life on the earth

The little planet which we call the earth is as a pinpoint on the map of the sky. In size it is very insignificant. But one fact distinguishes it from other heavenly bodies—it is so conditioned that life can exist on it. It is inhabited by intelligent beings, who are conscious of the mystery of things, who measure the stars and seek to know the Creator. The wonders of the earth and of man far surpass all the wonders of endless space.

When an astronomer through his telescope scans the sky, he finds everywhere unmistakable evidence of the handiwork of God, but he finds nowhere any evidence of the presence of creatures such as we. The popular idea of some years ago that Mars might be the home of persons like ourselves, and that the habitants of that planet had possibly seen the lights of the Chicago Exposition of 1892, and had attempted to signal us, is proved to be fancy rather than fact. On account of the absence of oxygen and hydrogen, there can be no water on Mars. Moreover, if water were supplied, the temperature would be too low for vegetable or animal life.

Similar conditions on other planets make life on them impossible. The climate on the moon runs to extremes. As it rotates on its axis the half turned from the sun is extremely cold: the half turned toward the sun becomes extremely hot. Under such conditions life cannot exist. Some of the planets are too near the sun, some are too far away, some revolve too slowly on their axes. "It is now generally agreed," says A. Cressy Morrison, in his excellent little book *Man Does Not Stand Alone,* "that there has never been, and never can be, life in any known form on any planet except our earth."

It is an arresting fact that here on this planet we call the earth is found a combination of conditions necessary for sustaining life—the seasons in order, the air we breathe, the temperature, the length of day and night, and other factors too numerous to mention. Here is a home made fit and ready for life of infinite variety, and for man in particular. When we remember that these conditions exist on no other planet, can we fail to wonder why it is so? The habitable earth is a fact that turns our grateful hearts to the Creator more than all the vastness and order of the sky!

We must not take our earth as a matter of course. How the elements and conditions necessary to life could be so brought together and adjusted is a mystery that baffles us. There is no explanation apart from belief in an intelligent and active God. I do not wonder that one of the greatest of our modern scientists should have said in recent years, "The universe begins to look more like a great thought than like a great machine." Or that Kepler, the astronomer, should have exclaimed, "I think God's thoughts after him."

In the preparation of the earth many factors are involved. Life is dependent on all of them—so much so that if one of them were upset this planet would be as void of living creatures as the moon. The earth moves in its orbit at a proper distance from the sun. If it were much nearer, its surface would be too hot; and if much farther, it would be too cold. If the earth were too near the moon, the ebb and flow of the tides would be so great that twice each day all the continents would be invaded by rushing waters and possibly destroyed by erosion. The earth is tilted on its axis at twenty-three degrees. Except for this provision, we would have no seasons, and as a result there would be, instead of teeming life, continents of ice and deserts. If our earth turned more slowly on its axis and our nights were three months long instead of twenty-four hours, nothing could survive.

The atmosphere enveloping the earth is indispensable. It is only a few miles in depth, and beyond it man cannot live except as oxygen and other elements necessary to sustaining life are mechanically provided. It is composed of the proper elements and in the right proportion to sustain life. We are especially dependent on oxygen. A sufficiency is stored in the crust of the earth and in the waters of the sea, and the supply is never diminished. The supply of oxygen in the air we breathe is adjusted to our needs more accurately than we can control the heat in our homes by a thermostat. If the proportion of oxygen in the atmosphere were twice as great as it is, the materials around us would be so inflammable that a stroke of lightning could change a continent to a roaring furnace. If the proportion of oxygen in the atmosphere were reduced by half, fire would not be possible.[1]

[1] For the form of statement in this and other paragraphs of this chapter, I acknowledge my indebtedness to A. Cressy Morrison, *Man Does Not Stand Alone* (Fleming H. Revell Co.).

Chance or intelligence

We need not multiply instances to illustrate how remarkable are the provisions on this planet for sustaining life. Every intelligent person, whether believer or atheist, must ask why or how all this came to be. There are only two possible answers—either by blind, unreasoning chance or by Infinite Intelligence. Between chance and intelligence, I take my stand with intelligence. I must.

The possibility that the planet on which we live could have been prepared for us and all living things by chance is so remote that it does not exist. A simple problem in mathematics should make this clear:

Take ten pennies and mark them 1 to 10. Put them in your pocket and give them a good shake. Now, try to draw them out in succession, 1 to 10, each in its regular order, putting each coin back in your pocket after each draw. Your chance of drawing No. 1 first is 1 to 10. Your chance of drawing No. 1 and No. 2 in succession would be 1 to 100. Your chance of drawing No. 1 to No. 10 in succession, each in its regular order, is one chance in 10,000,000,000.[2]

Many more than ten conditions, each in its proper order and each fitting into the others, are necessary to make the earth habitable—light, climate, atmosphere, food supply, and the like. One day I counted twenty-five such conditions and provisions, and this by no means exhausts the list. Reverting to our problem, if you should attempt to draw twenty-five pennies, marked No. 1 to No. 25, one

[2] Quoted with slight variations from Morrison.

after the other and each in its regular order, the chances against it are so enormous that the figures are beyond us. Let the reader try raising 25 to the 25th power, and see for himself.

"So many essential conditions are necessary for life to exist on our earth," says Morrison, "that it is mathematically impossible that all of them could exist in proper relationship by chance on any one earth at one time."

Mathematics is against the theory of chance. Common sense is against it. We know that if it were possible for one to throw up a handful of glass and steel and gold every second for a million years, it would never come down a watch. A watch requires a designer and maker. No less do the numerous and various provisions on the earth point conclusively to a wise and active Creator. "The fool hath said in his heart, There is no God." We are on solid scientific as well as religious ground when we declare, "I believe in God . . . , Maker of heaven and earth."

Order in every detail

The evidences of divine care and wisdom are seen in the smallest details of the natural order as clearly as in the widest spaces. In laboratories and in open fields one may read "the manuscripts of God." The microscope reveals wonders in nature's design as amazing as may ever be discerned through the telescope. Within an atom, too small to be seen through the strongest microscope, is stored an incredible power. Scientists have at long last learned to split it, and the possibilities of atomic energy amaze and terrify us. The movements of protons and electrons within the atom are as baffling as the movements of the stars.

Chemical elements combine with each other by dependable laws—laws that every chemist knows. Two parts of hydrogen and one of oxygen brought together produce water at any time and anywhere. Ask nature the same question in the same way and she will always give you the same answer. On this principle every scientist depends in his search for truth, and he is never disappointed.

When I was a little lad my mother showed me one day how every leaf of the boxwood hedge that lined our walkway was made in two layers, fastened together only on the edges. It was my first lesson in the Creator's design and care in every detail of his handiwork.

> . . . . . . The fool
> Contends that God is not—
> Not God! in gardens! when the eve is cool?
> Nay, but I have a sign;
> 'Tis very sure God walks in mine.

Every leaf of every tree and shrub is fashioned after its own particular pattern—the petals of every flower unfold in orderly beauty—the bees build the honeycomb with unexcelled skill—and birds, after long winter migrations, guided over land and sea by a strange power, return to last summer's nests. Everywhere we discover the fingerprints of the Almighty—everywhere the undeniable proof of his care and providence!

Feelings too deep for words

Through its order and its mystery, in its vastness and in every smallest detail, all nature is an unanswerable proof of an intelligent Creator who is God. No less impressively nature reflects "the beauty of the Lord our God." Enfolded in her great arms, as when we stroll alone through a forest, or in pensive mood look upon her grandeur and her indescribable loveliness, our hearts experience a joy too deep for words. Fields and forests, sea and sky seem to be the garments of the Almighty, the visible vesture of his invisible Spirit, and we are impressed by a sense of his presence.

I do not think of such experiences as moments of fancy, but rather as moments of insight. Our intuitions may be more reliable than our logic. At such times we catch the meaning of Wordsworth's exquisite lines:

> I have felt
> A presence that disturbs me with the joy
> Of elevated thoughts; a sense sublime
> Of something far more deeply interfused,
> Whose dwelling is the light of setting suns,
> And the round ocean and the living air,
> And the blue sky, and in the mind of man.

A radiant spring morning, a forest in autumn, a sunrise at sea, the starlit sky, the intimate beauty of one's own garden—all these are ways by which the Master Artist makes known to us the beauty that is in him. The response of our hearts assures us of our kinship to him. A lover of nature has in his soul a spark of the divine. A distinguished botanist once said, after watching the unfolding of an unpretentious flower, "I saw God in his glory pass near me, and bowed my head in worship."

I sat with friends one morning on the deck of a ship to watch the sunrise. The ship's nurse came out and, leaning on the rail, watched with us the indescribable sight. When, at last, the sun was up, she turned to us and said with rare reverence and awe, "I watch it every morning, and each morning it is different." And a quiet reverence rested upon our little company like that one feels in the worship of the sanctuary. The great open spaces, where nature is seen in all her variant moods, are, as Longfellow says, "the roofless temple of God." There he is ever present to reverent and understanding hearts. There one may almost overhear the harmonies of the choir invisible, singing the first lines of the *Te Deum:*

> We praise Thee, O God; we acknowledge
> Thee to be the Lord.
> All the earth doth worship Thee, the
> Father everlasting.

The order and beauty of creation must convince any reasonable inquirer that the Creator is a Being of infinite intelligence and beauty, whose power no man can measure. But nature is not our only teacher concerning God. Indeed, it is not our principal teacher. Within our hearts are questions and yearnings for which nature offers no adequate answer. We ask, What is the place and worth of the individual in God's great design?—or, more pointedly, Does God care for me? We yearn for a sense of security amid the changes of time, for an assurance of the final triumph of right in a world of sin and tragedy, for present fellowship with God and continuing life in him beyond "our bourne of Time and Place." Concerning these more intimate and personal longings, nature speaks no assuring word.

But God reveals himself in many ways, and in our search for him we turn to other spheres of life and action where he is yet more manifest.

CHAPTER III

GOD IN MAN

"NOT NATURE BUT HUMAN NATURE IS GOD'S BEST REvealer." Only a person can adequately interpret another person. Since God is a person he is revealed in man more clearly than in all the laws and wonders of the physical universe. In our search for him we, therefore, turn from nature to human nature—to ourselves.

Often have I looked with admiration on the nation's capitol in Washington. When entering the city, I watch for the first sight of its stately dome. We know that such an impressive pile of brick and stone would not be except for the architect who planned its every part. The completed building is undeniable proof of his intelligence and skill. But, for all that, the architect is to us a vague and distant person. The structure which he so skillfully planned reveals to us nothing of his personal character. Was he a friendly soul in whose company we would find delight? What joys and sorrows were crowded into his years? The noble structure he designed does not answer. These more personal traits are not disclosed in architectural lines.

One who confines his search for God to nature's grand

design cannot really know him. Science has its limitations, as the best scientists are continually telling us. Test tubes cannot disclose the hopes and passions of the soul. A chemist may analyze a tear, but the sorrow of the heart behind the tear is beyond the reach of chemistry. An astronomer once exclaimed, "I have searched the heavens, and have not found God." Did he not know that God could not be found through a telescope? By the aid of his glass he may discern the architecture of the universe, but not the Architect.

Spiritual truth belongs to the sphere of the personal, and therefore in the life of man we find the deeper and more intimate manifestations of God. The Bible's first declaration concerning man is that he is made in God's image— that is, he thinks and loves and wills, as God does. For this reason God's thoughts and purposes are reflected in man's aspiring soul and in his long history on the earth more impressively than in all the order and beauty of creation.

Man's yearning for God

A great need usually implies that there is somewhere a provision for supplying it. In the world as we find it, need and satisfaction answer each the other. We must have food, and it is provided. Our souls love the beautiful—and behold the earth and the sky! Love requires fellowship, and "God setteth the solitary in families." Above all, man needs God. Life is incomplete without him, and in every soul there is an insatiate hunger for the divine. This at least suggests that he who created the need has made provision for its satisfaction.

Man's deepest yearning is for God. It is persistent and universal. "Man shall not live by bread alone," nor by all the things he may possess. Neither riches nor pleasure nor achievement can of themselves satisfy our aspiring souls. A psalmist looks into his own inner life and reveals to us his deepest need and ours: "As the hart panteth after the water brooks, so panteth my soul after thee, O God." The cry of Job is caught up by all the races of men: "Oh that I knew where I might find him! that I might come even to his seat!" All this is another way of saying that man is intuitively and persistently religious. Only the divine can satisfy the heart's deepest longing—only God can fill its vacancies.

It is an impressive fact that wherever man is, in every age and in every place, he is reaching out for God. A universal intuition cannot be false! No tribe or race, however primitive, has been found that did not have some idea of God, some form of worship though often crude. Some of the religions of heathenism are depraving in the extreme. They teach their followers to worship reptiles or stones, and sometimes give approval and blessing to their basest impulses. Their errors and superstitions have for generations imprisoned men in mental and spiritual darkness. Other faiths have in them elements of solid truth and some clear insights into the ways of the Almighty, and yet they are woefully incomplete and insufficient. Notwithstanding the tragedy and incompleteness of pagan faiths, they at least reveal one impressive fact—the insistent cry of the human heart for God—

> Like plants in mines which never saw the sun
> But dream of him, and guess where he may be,
> And do their best to climb and get to him.

All of them might make their own the pathetic words of a singer in Israel, "My heart and my flesh crieth out for the living God." Like the men of Athens, they seek the Unknown God.

Our hearts are drawn to God as steel is pulled toward a magnet. An atheist may deny him, but in his better moments he is conscious of a strange tug at his heart. A Marxian communist refuses to believe in Deity, and then makes a god of the state and is restless and unhappy in his man-made religion. Tyrants and dictators may for a while suppress religion, but soon it surges back—even in Russia.

Belief in God is as much a part of a child's intuition as love for his parents. Helen Keller, blind and deaf from infancy, was entrusted by her father to Bishop Phillips Brooks for religious instruction. When he spoke to her of God, she answered out of physical darkness and silence: "I have always known there was a God, but I have never before known his name."

I know that the universal heart of man is not drawn to—*nothing*. For centuries man did not understand the ebb and flow of the tides. At last he learned that the moon disturbs the waters of all the seas, and that the tides are made by the moon's attraction. As the moon pulls the waters of the great deep, so God draws all men to himself. This tug at our hearts is as unmistakable as the force of gravitation. It is beyond the realm of the physical, and yet none the less real. It disturbs and urges us. It is proof of a great reality beyond us and above us, and that reality is God.

Conscience

In the breast of each of us is a voice which we call conscience. No one can define it, and yet everyone is conscious of it. Guided by this inner light we are able to distinguish between right and wrong. It is, like the heart's hunger for God, a universal gift. All persons possess at least an elemental sense of right, and respect it.

Conscience speaks, and one who dares to disregard its voice reaps distress and disaster. If he attempts to flee from it, it tracks him down like the hounds of hell. No accuser at the bar is so relentless as one's own conscience. Accused by it, David prays, "Have mercy upon me, O God . . . I have sinned." Under its lashing Judas brings back to the chief priests the price of his treachery and hangs himself. Condemned by it Lady Macbeth, in delirium, cries: "What, will these hands ne'er be clean?"

What is this thing we call conscience? Is it a reflex of our own ideas, or does it come from a source beyond ourselves? I am sure it is not of our making. We cannot control it, and we cannot escape it. We do not command it: it commands us. As all creation bears witness to the orderliness and wisdom of God, so conscious bears witness to his unchanging righteousness. It speaks with more than human authority. When we violate it, we suffer a sense of guilt which we cannot throw off. A little boy overtaken in a falsehood said, "I despise myself." An elderly man, esteemed and respected, came to my study one day to confess a sin of his youth, the memory of which had haunted all his days.

Conscience persuades us to do what no earthly power can. For conscience' sake Moses "refused to be called the son of Pharaoh's daughter; choosing rather to suffer affliction with the people of God." Supported by a good conscience, Paul spoke boldly and confidently before Agrippa, and Luther at the Diet of Worms challenged the entrenched power of Europe with the words, "I can do none other."

The history of conscience is the story of the race's upward march. As long as man has been on the earth this inner voice has restrained him from acts base and unworthy, and urged him "to do justly, and to love mercy." I doubt not that conscience is the warning and pleading of God.

"Labor to keep alive in your breast," wrote George Washington, "that little spark of celestial fire called Conscience." It is light out of the spiritual world. Its source is God. It could not have evolved out of anything in the natural order, for nature, "red in tooth and claw," does not have it. Neither is it a kind of glorified self-interest. Rather, on account of it, men have renounced themselves, their comforts and securities, and ventured forth as crusaders for the truth. "They were stoned, . . . were sawn asunder, . . . were slain with the sword: . . . being destitute, afflicted, tormented."

Through conscience, the God of infinite spaces speaks directly to each of us. We cannot explain it apart from God. We can find no peace except by obeying its voice. We who live under its authority see behind it and pervading it "a power not ourselves making for righteousness." Who can live with his conscience and deny God?

The trail of the centuries

The ways and purposes of God are as evident in the story of the race as in the experience of the individual.

The history of man on the earth has been from one point of view a story of blood and tears. How hard has been his struggle for freedom and the abundant life! How tragic have been his mistakes, and how many his reverses! How frequently in this long story right has been on the scaffold and wrong on the throne!

And yet one is blind, indeed, who does not discern amid the tragedies of history the slow and persistent progress of mankind. The age-long experience of humanity is much like the personal trials of Paul who, in the midst of his tempestuous career, wrote of himself, "perplexed, but not in despair, . . . cast down, but not destroyed." We suffer temporary defeats—

Yet I doubt not through the ages one increasing purpose runs,
And the thoughts of men are widened with the process of
the suns.

This is not a mere bit of poetic optimism. It is solid fact. History is the story of God's dealings with man, and his progress, though interrupted by many recessions, is too evident to require argument.

Recorded history covers a period of some six thousand years. Along that highway man has moved slowly but surely to higher ground, with occasional and sometimes tragic dips into the valley. At the dawn of history tyrants ruled and the unnumbered masses were little more than "dumb, driven cattle." The centuries have demonstrated that man has within him a spark of the divine. He recognizes, though often unconsciously, his kinship to God, and refuses to be the tool of tyrants, or the slave of human systems.

At the beginning the race was divided into warring clans, and in that primitive society might was right. With the passing of time a different pattern has appeared. States have been organized, laws have been codified, and human rights and dignities are winning a slow but certain victory. The oppressed and the forgotten are demanding for themselves a chance, and a share in the good things that Providence has provided. Today we think in terms of a federated and warless world—not yet achieved, but the dream is in our souls and the idea is embodied in a covenant of nations.

What the future holds none can foretell, but that the trek of mankind has been along an upward way none can deny. I am sure that all this has not come to pass by chance or by the interplay of mere human forces. I can find no adequate explanation except in the control of a righteous and sovereign God. I cannot doubt that

. . . . behind the dim unknown,
Standeth God within the shadow, keeping watch above his own.

The wicked have sometimes flourished like a green bay tree, but God has never permitted the wickedness of man to destroy his world. I am sure he never will, not even with an atomic bomb. He has set limits to man's iniquity, as he has set bounds to the sea. When a nation has reached the extreme of pride and sensuousness and oppression, it disintegrates and falls of its own weight, and another is raised up. The story has been repeated many times in the rise and fall of empires. God is in control, and nothing endures that is contrary to his sovereign love and righteousness.

In these later years, leadership has fallen to our western world. If we fail, God will not be defeated. He will pass his banners to other hands! History is a record of God's judgments, and by it we are taught that in spite of man's wickedness God is active in his world. There is a core of solemn truth in the somewhat irreverent lines—

> You'll have to get up early
> To get ahead of God.

Recorded history teaches another lesson that we greatly need to take to heart. The periods when the rights and dignity of man have been recognized, when democratic states have been born, and freedom and hope have flourished—these have been periods when men have believed most resolutely in God. Religion is the pillar that supports a just and brotherly society. Our western civilization has in it many unchristian elements, but it was organized and built around belief in the reality of God and the moral law.

There are among us some who assume that religion may be discarded in this age of science, and that we shall still be able to retain the blessings and benefits which Christianity originally brought to our civilization—democracy, family life, a moral conscience, and the inherent right of every man to life, liberty, and happiness. But this can be done no more than one traveling on a dark road can keep the light after he has thrown his lantern away. "If the foundations be destroyed, what can the righteous do?" I have no hope for the recovery of civilization except by a revival of faith in God. Should we in our blindness discard religion and depend solely on the ingenuity of politicians and industrialists, the disaster will become worse.

Our condition will be as Samson's when he overturned the supporting pillars in the temple of Dagon and the whole structure tumbled upon his defenseless head.

The soul's experience of God

God becomes most real in the intimate experiences of the individual with him. Moses became conscious of his presence beside a bush in Horeb. The youthful Isaiah in the temple was suddenly made aware of him. Paul had a like experience on the road to Damascus, and his remaining years were lived in the afterglow of that hour. In each instance a man was so moved by a Presence and a Power that he dedicated himself to do the will of One who had spoken to him. Such experiences are what Wordsworth calls "the divine hour." God invades the life of an individual, and becomes as real to him as a friend in flesh and blood.

Augustine once said that he had searched the world for God, and found him in his heart. A great cloud of witnesses, the noblest and best of men, tell us out of their own experience that

> . . . . . Spirit with Spirit can meet—
> Closer is He than breathing, and nearer than
> hands and feet.

At the age of twenty-two, Charles Kingsley recorded in his Journal: "I have been for the last hour on the seashore, not dreaming but thinking deeply and strongly. . . . Before the sleeping earth and the sleepless sea and stars I have devoted myself to God." |

During World War II, a young fellow wrote me from the far Pacific: "As I sit here watching the relentless surf pound our reef, I cannot see a thing that is not run by God's own hand. . . . He rules our lives from birth to death kindly. . . . There is nothing to fear." R. W. Dale tells of a friend who, lying on the side of a hill, was overwhelmed by the beauty of the scene that stretched before him. "And then suddenly," he said, "through all that I saw there came the very glory of God. I knew that he was there. His presence, his power, and his goodness took possession of me and held me." Teresa of Avila, great mystic and founder of an order in the Roman Church, wrote, "In prayer there would sometimes come to me such a sense of the presence of God that I seemed to be engulfed in him."

So along life's way the individual meets God, face to face —or better, soul to soul. Sometimes the experience comes when we are in prayer or worship. It may come as we pass through a valley of deep sorrow, or when our hearts are glad, or when we are engaged in some kindly ministry or menial task. I once heard Rufus Jones, of Haverford College, relate that during some weeks of confinement when he was recovering from an accident he was suddenly lifted into a glowing sense of God's reality hitherto unknown to him. These experiences are beyond the reach of test tubes

and microscopes. The reality that is within us finds the
Reality that is beyond us—and we know!

> Lord of all being, throned afar,
> Thy glory flames from sun and star;
> Center and soul of every sphere,
> Yet to each loving heart how near!

CHAPTER IV

GOD IN CHRIST

A HIGH-CASTE INDIAN ONE DAY ASKED E. STANLEY JONES how God could be made real to him. Dr. Jones gave the inquirer a copy of the New Testament and said: "If you will read a portion of this book every day at an appointed hour, and then will listen quietly to the voice of the Spirit, I will guarantee that within the course of six months God will become a reality to you." Later a satisfied inquirer returned to say that it had turned out as Dr. Jones had promised.

God discovered in a Book! "Thy word is a lamp unto my feet, and a light unto my path." The New Testament tells the story of Jesus Christ. He is its radiant center, its shining light. The burden of its message is that in Christ God has come to the level of our understanding and experience. "The Word was made flesh, and dwelt among us, and we beheld his glory." Christ is God's own answer to the yearning and questioning heart of man—and it is better than any that human wisdom can devise.

God's supreme revelation of himself is Jesus Christ. This is the central and distinctive teaching of the Christian faith. It is the "good news" that the Church has carried into every part of the world through these nineteen hundred years. Other religions tell the story of man's persistent and sometimes tragic search for God. Christianity is the story of God's search for man. "Show us the Father and we will be satisfied," said Philip to his Master on the night that Jesus and the twelve met in the Upper Room. Then came the reply from the lips of Jesus: "He that hath seen me hath seen the Father." In creation we find the fingerprints of God. In the soul of man are broken reflections of the Infinite One, as the broken reflection of the moon on the river's bosom. In Christ God is manifest in human form. Most of all, we believe in God because a Man once lived in Galilee!

The fact of Christ

More than once in these brief studies reference has been made to the amazing wonders of creation. But no wonder on the earth or in the sky is comparable to Jesus Christ. He was a member of a minority race. He was born of a peasant mother. He grew to manhood in a disreputable crossroads town in an obscure provice of the Empire. During his lifetime he was never more than a hundred miles from the place of his birth. And yet this Person has so affected the life of mankind that we date a new era from the year of his birth. He walks amid the centuries, and they are divided into B.C. and A.D. We do not write a letter to a friend or a check for a creditor without recording that it has been so many years since Jesus was born.

The character of Jesus has become humanity's ideal. Even Pilate, who consented to his death, said of him, "I find no fault in him." Believer and unbeliever alike honor the excellence of his character. His life reveals the possibilities that are in man, and we have made him our pattern. We can pay no higher tribute to another than to say he is Christlike. The teachings of Jesus have so captured the mind of the world that men of all nations and parties are saying that there is no hope for this desperate age except by the way of the Golden Rule and brotherhood and good will. For every one who reads the classics of ancient Greece and Rome, there are tens of thousands who read the words of Jesus. Ernest Renan, brilliant skeptic of the nineteenth century, ends his *Life of Jesus* with a glowing tribute to him: "Whatever may be the surprises of the future," he says, "Jesus will never be surpassed."

When in his early thirties, Jesus was condemned and executed as a disturber of the peace. But after Good Friday came Easter Day and the Resurrection. His disciples testify that he appeared to them, and certainly these men who had lived in intimate fellowship with the Teacher of all teachers were men of honor. They became the interpreters of a crucified and risen Christ, and the greatest movement of all time was begun.

The influence of Jesus has changed the course of history. It has given to mankind a new awareness of God, and a new sense of human worth and dignity. The wonder of all wonders is Christ! His followers—of whom I am one—receive him as the divine Son of God. We never think of him as dead. For nineteen centuries the best men on the earth have testified that he has been to them a living Presence, a companion of every way, in whose fellowship they have come to know God for a surety and by whose strange power their lives have been transformed. I do not understand how one can claim to be an educated person who is not acquainted with the New Testament record of such a life as this, and with the story of his continuing and increasing power over mankind. And how can any earnest seeker after God fail to linger at the feet of the Teacher from Nazareth?

We come to the very heart of our study when we ask what Jesus teaches concerning God.

> Hushed be the noise and the strife of the schools,
> Volume and pamphlet, sermon and speech,
> The lips of the wise and the prattle of fools.
> Let the Son of Man teach!

Jesus of Nazareth speaks

The most outstanding fact in the life of Jesus is his awareness of God. He did not argue—he lived in the radiance of the Father's presence. His first recorded saying is his question to his mother and Joseph, "Did ye not know that I must be about my Father's business?" At the end he prayed, "Father, into thy hands I commend my spirit." His awareness of God is so unstudied and assuring that it is contagious. We cannot read one of the Gospels with open

46

and reverent mind but the same awareness is awakened in us.

Jesus saw in nature's endless panorama infallible signs of the Father's wisdom and care. In his teachings there is none of the smell of a laboratory, nor the formality of a classroom. His words rather are characterized by spiritual intuition and insight, more incisive and trustworthy than all our worldly wisdom. We recognize the truthfulness of his simple words as we recognize the glorious beauty of a spring morning, or the harmonies of a symphony. His teachings are flashes of light by which we are able to see the truth, as in an instant, and the plain path along which we may walk.

The Man of Galilee recognized in the wild lilies of Galilee, more beautiful than any kingly splendor, the work of the divine Artist. Bird and beast are objects of God's care and providence. "Your heavenly Father feedeth them," and not a sparrow falls without his notice. A strange power stirs within the planted seed, and at the season's end a field of golden grain appears—"ye know not how." Jesus saw in the process a demonstration of God's gentle power. Before science had spoken so eloquently of an all-enveloping order and of the mystery of life, Jesus had perceived at the heart of things the care of a wise and benevolent Father. A scientist uses different terms, but science nonetheless confirms the teaching of Jesus, that an intelligent Power beyond the natural order sustains all things. That power is God.

Jesus, more than any man who ever lived, has taught us to find the mind and heart of God reflected in the soul of man. God, he said, is like a man who during a long absence trusted his estate to his employees and held each responsible for the use he made of it. He is like a faithful shepherd who searches the wilderness for one lost sheep. In his greatest parable God is portrayed as a father whose love followed a wicked son into the shambles of shame, and at the end welcomed the repentant boy home.

Our Lord had high regard for the worth and dignity of man. No humanist in ancient or modern times approaches Jesus in his regard for human personality. But God, he said, must be infinitely better than the best and wisest of men. The creature cannot excel the Creator. "If ye then, being evil, know how to give good gifts unto your children, *how much more* shall your Father which is in heaven give good things to them that ask him?" All the virtues of man are inescapable proof of the greater goodness of God.

The Son of God taught mankind to pray, "Our Father which art in heaven." He said that the human race is as one family in which God is our Father, and we are all brothers. What simplicity sublime! And yet how profound! Our Lord's simple phrases point the only way by which the antagonisms of nations and races may be healed, and a new world order achieved. Father and brother—these everyday words are the key to the mystery of God and the redemption of society. As we linger over our Lord's teachings concerning the Heavenly Father, we find them satisfying as bread to a hungry man. The arms of the Eternal enfold us, a light shines along our path, and a song is in our heart.

God with us

What Jesus was has deeper meaning than what he said. An Old Testament prophet, dreaming of a deliverer to come, calls him "Immanuel," which in the Hebrew tongue means "God with us." In the person of Jesus, "the everlasting God, . . . the Creator of the ends of the earth," has come to the level of our human life and understanding.

God in Christ has come out of the everywhere into the here. He has stepped out of the mysteries, and reveals himself as Father and Friend of man.

In this brief discussion we do not attempt to explore the mystery of the divinity of Jesus Christ. But the facts forbid that we classify him as mere man. We need to learn the reasons which the theologians give for the Church's age-long faith in his divine nature. But the Christian's belief in our Lord's divinity is not proved so much by treatise and argument as by our association with him in the bonds of faith and obedience. The disciples who companied with him in the days of his flesh discovered that they were in the presence of God. Peter one day exclaimed as if by divine intuition, "Thou art the Christ, the Son of the living God." Thomas, doubting and melancholy man, at last con-

49

fessed, "My Lord and my God." Jesus was for them more than a demonstration of God. He was God.

One of Paul's most trenchant phrases is *"in Christ."* In his letter to the Ephesians, this phrase or its equivalent is repeated more than twenty times. It describes the vital union between a genuine Christian and the Lord Jesus. We may live in the glow of his presence and fellowship, and soon we discover that we are in the presence and fellowship of God. No wonders revealed by science or arguments of philosophers are so convincing as one's experience of God in Christ. Through Christ the "Creator of heaven and earth" becomes to us Immanuel—"God with us." Not by merely accepting a creed, but by living daily in his fellowship—not out of a calculating intellect, but out of a warm heart and faithful obedience to his word— only thus do we learn the inward meaning of one of the Church's most ancient hymns:

> Thou art the King of glory, O Christ.
> Thou art the everlasting Son of the Father.
>
> .   .   .   .
>
> Day by day, we magnify thee.
> And we worship thy name ever, world without end.
>
> .   .   .   .
>
> O Lord, in thee have I trusted; let me never
> be confounded.

Near the end of the gospel story stands a cross. God's dear Son "suffered under Pontius Pilate, was crucified, dead, and buried." These words from the Apostles' Creed have a sound of dreadful finality. But instead, the death of Jesus discloses in an incomparable way the depth and extent of the love of God. The cross is accepted by believers the world over—whether Roman Catholic, or Orthodox, or Protestant—as Christianity's most adequate and persuasive symbol.

We can in a measure understand the Master's plain teaching concerning the wisdom and providence of God. We recognize in his pure and devoted life a demonstration of the divine nature. But what does his death on a cross reveal concerning God? This at least—it reveals God's suffering concern for his world and the length to which he goes to save all men from sin and fear. As Carlyle tells us in forceful phrases, God has not wound up his universe and then retired to a secluded heaven to watch it spin.

God loves to the utmost the races of men he has created in his image. He will not abandon them. He suffers to cure sin's hurt, to rescue us from frustration and tragedy, and to set our feet in the way of everlasting life. Whatever is necessary for our forgiveness and redemption, God has done through Jesus Christ. When love suffers it becomes redemptive. When we look upon that strange Man upon his cross we behold a love that we cannot fathom. Committing to him the things that are beyond our power—the sins of our yesterdays and all the doubts and fears that harrass us—we are made conscious of sins forgiven and the incoming of a new life. It is the action of the love of God in Jesus Christ. We call it the new birth.

At the center of the Christian's faith stands Jesus Christ. Of himself he said, "I and my Father are one," and "No man cometh unto the Father, but by me." Of him Paul wrote: "God, who commanded the light to shine out of darkness, hath shined in our hearts, to give the light of the knowledge of the glory of God in the face of Jesus Christ." Let every seeker after God linger over the story of Jesus of Nazareth, and commit himself to him as a faithful disciple, and God will become to such an one as real as the sunlight. Robert Browning, humble follower and rare interpreter of Christ, nowhere gave surer proof of his understanding than when he wrote:

> The acknowledgment of God in Christ
> Accepted by thy reason, solves for thee
> All questions in the earth and out of it.

CHAPTER V

FAITH IS THE KEY

CHRISTIANITY HAS A MESSAGE. IT SPEAKS A STRONG, assuring word concerning God. With bold confidence it affirms that he is, that he is in control of his creation, and that he is solicitous for the well-being of all men. We who are the objects of his care may rely on his wisdom and trust his lovingkindness.

The evidences of God are overwhelming and final. We have reviewed a few of them and find that God is inescapable. Every person who senses the meaning of the world and the yearnings of his own heart may say with an ancient psalmist, "Whither shall I flee from thy presence? . . . If I take the wings of the morning, and dwell in the uttermost parts of the sea; even there shall thy hand lead me, and thy right hand shall hold me."

Christianity also has a purpose. What it has to say about God and man is not a mere theory which scholars may examine at their leisure. Neither is it an incidental interest which worldly people may discuss over their teacups as they discuss fashions and markets and politics. It is a teaching of immediate concern, vitally related to all that we are and hope to be. The purpose of the Christian message is to lift every individual to such an assurance of God that his mind may be convinced, his heart at peace, and his life transformed.

How may one obtain this boon and blessing? How may mortal man live in conscious and saving fellowship with the eternal God? The answer is not discovered by accident or won by some grand achievement. It is found by an attitude of mind and heart, by an approach to life and God that the Bible calls *faith*.

Two words, often repeated in the New Testament, set forth more clearly than any other the inner meaning of the Christian religion—"grace" and "faith." "Grace" defies all definition. It stands in the Bible as a kind of symbol of God's lovingkindness. It "is love with a mysterious plus." It is love in action, moving out to help and bless another without asking whether he is worthy. It is love freely giving itself. Grace is the sum of all the unmerited favors which the Father bestows upon us. It describes a quality of life so divine and magnificent that we do not speak of the grace of man, but only of the grace of God.

"Faith," on the other hand, describes a human act and attitude. In the Bible it stands for man's response to God's grace. *"By* grace are ye saved *through faith."* Faith, therefore, is the key that unlocks for every person who will use it the door that admits him into the divine fellowship and to the abundant life which God so freely offers.

Possibly no word in our common speech has been so

persistently misunderstood as "faith." Some have thought of it as a blind guess, as when one leaps in the dark not knowing whether he is on the edge of a precipice or of a garden lawn. Others have spoken of faith as empty sentiment, or as a refuge for fools and defeated persons. Still others have regarded it as cold and formal assent to a creed. One misguided cynic said, "Faith is believing what you know is not so."

On the contrary, "faith" as used in the New Testament is a great word, rich and all-inclusive, describing the response of mind and emotion and will to the appeal of God. Since the Bible lays such large emphasis on faith as the means by which God becomes a reality to any who will exercise it, it is therefore worth our time and effort to learn what its real meaning is.

Faith is belief

Faith in God is not a fancy suspended in thin air. It rests on the foundation of what one genuinely believes to be true concerning God and man's relation to him.

Every day, in every phase of our activity, we live by what we believe to be true and trustworthy. A scientist must believe in natural law. Indeed, all science rests on the solid belief that the physical world is governed by unchanging laws which we may discover and use to our benefit. A man sows his fields in the belief that nature will not fail him, and that autumn will bring him harvests of ripened grain. A woman gives her heart and hand in the bonds of holy wedlock because she believes in the man of her choice. Marriage that does not rest on the confidence of two persons, the one in the other, has no enduring foundation.

Genuine religion is belief in the reality of God and of the spiritual world. A creedless religion is as unthinkable as lawless science. Faith does not grow in a vacuum. We can never achieve a knowledge of God by chasing question marks, or by yielding ourselves to be tossed about by every wind of doubt. "He that cometh to God must believe that he is, and that he is a rewarder of them that diligently seek him."

The proofs of God's wisdom, his care for his world, and his unfolding purposes are so evident and convincing that I am unable to understand how one can be intellectually respectable and deny that he is. Indeed, I have never known a thoroughgoing atheist. When we think on the material universe, planned and controlled in every detail —vast, dependable, beautiful—we cannot escape belief in a great First Cause. The end of atheism is an intellectual black-out. The aspirations of man, his response to truth and right, the sweet mystery of life—all these unmistakably point us to the Source of love and truth, as every sunbeam tells us there is a sun. The excellence of Jesus Christ, the increasing power of his Spirit in the world, and his presence in the hearts of all his followers are facts as undeniable as the air we breathe.

We may magnify our doubts. This is a negative attitude.

It leads us nowhere. Belief must be positive. Let one seize upon what he does believe of the Christian teaching concerning God, and start from that point. I have yet to know a person who did not have sufficient belief in God to begin with, if only he would follow through. Then let him begin with what he can believe and from that point build his faith. Let him search earnestly for the truth of God in creation and in man. Let him saturate his mind with the truths of the Bible, and let him keep company with men who know God and whose daily lives reflect his goodness. And, above all, let him live daily by all the light he has. So every individual may build his temple of faith, resting on the foundation of strong convictions. The truth concerning God, as all other truth, does not come unsought. It must be achieved. One who nurses his doubts, or halts by his unbelief, cannot achieve it.

No adventure so challenges the whole mind and spirit of man as that which calls him to learn the truth concerning God. This is faith's beginning.

Faith is commitment

Faith is more than belief. Mere belief may become a sterile, lifeless thing. A creed by itself may degenerate into cant. Faith is belief plus a venture. It is a creed in action. It is the commitment of one's all to God in whom he believes. So Paul, writing of the faith that had strengthened him for every task and which supported him as he was about to pass through the gates of death, says, "I know whom *I have believed,* and am persuaded that he is able to keep that which *I have committed* unto him against that day."

Belief blossoms into commitment and a venture, and a man of faith emerges. Herein lies the chief cause of our spiritual blindness. It is not so much on account of our unbelief that we fail in our quest for God as our failure to commit ourselves to what we actually believe. One knows in the deeps of his soul that behind the mysterious universe is One infinitely wise and dependable. He cannot escape the tug of the divine at his heart.

Of all the persons who through the years have come to discuss with me the Christian faith, not one has denied his belief in a Supreme Being by whose power a beautiful and ordered world came into existence. But many have failed to act on that belief. They did not humble themselves before his majesty, or praise him for his excellent goodness. How many are they who, believing in a Supreme Being, refuse to commit themselves to his wisdom, and to trust him to do for them what they are not able to do for themselves! In their thinking and living they ignore him, and their years are beset by questions and fears—not because they have blotted God out of their intellectual sky, but because they have refused to commit themselves to him. No belief in God becomes a saving power in one's life until he commits himself to it, and ventures to live by it.

We believe that God has revealed himself in Jesus Christ, and then we resolutely say, "Where he leads me I will follow." We believe that God draws near us in his Son, and then we give ourselves to him in fellowship and service. We believe in forgiveness, and throw ourselves on divine mercy. Faith is belief plus decision and action.

R. S. Barrett tells the story of a brilliant young surgeon who devised a new method for operating on the brain. He submitted his plan to his fellow physicians, and they approved it. They believed in him and his skill. A few days later a man rang the young physician's doorbell and said: "I am an ill man. I am stricken with a malady of the brain. I have learned of you, and I have come to trust myself to you and your skill." The first was belief; the second was faith. When in one's religious experience belief becomes commitment the fair flower of faith appears, making fragrant all the gardens of the soul.

Faith is assurance

The inner assurance of God is faith's crowning glory. When we speak of an indescribable assurance which dawns upon the mind of man like morning's light, we are in the company of mystics and poets rather than of logicians. It is a certitude beyond the framework of argument or scientific proof, more intuition than pure reason. It is an insight rather than an intellectual achievement—as when an artist perceives beauty, or a musician suddenly becomes aware of sweet harmonies and composes a symphony. Of this aspect of faith the author of Hebrews was writing when he said that faith "is assurance of things hoped for, a conviction of things not seen." This inner certitude is our unfailing surety, as real as conscience and more trustworthy than physical sight. "The Spirit itself beareth witness with our spirit," and we know with an assurance beyond all questioning.

Across the ages the gentlest and the most heroic have, like Moses, "endured, as seeing him who is invisible." An unfaltering assurance of God and his goodness is not a figment of the imagination, for in its strength unnumbered thousands have "subdued kingdoms, wrought righteousness," and faced a martyr's death rather than deny its reality. It has been described as a "sixth sense"—the faculty to perceive truth that lies beyond the physical senses—wonders which "eye hath not seen, nor ear heard." When achieved it is clearer than all our studied reasoning and stronger than all our doubts.

Tennyson describes faith's assurance as "a warmth within the breast." What the mind accepts as true and trustworthy concerning God, the heart may joyfully experience. The inward peace is our final proof. In spite of tyrants and cynics, religion continues to be a mighty force because there is an unnumbered multitude of men and women in every part of the world, many of them obscure and unlettered, who have by faith found their way into the secret of God's presence. For them he is as near and real as one's most intimate friend. They carry in their souls an assurance that the intellect cannot analyze.

Such assurance may be attained by any who walk by

faith in God. Old doubts and frustrations may sometimes return to vex us. But if we continue in the way, believe in the wisdom and goodness of God and venture to live each day by that belief, we will arrive. As a gospel hymn puts it, "trust and obey," and the inward assurance will become our joyous conviction.

When a person's faith has lifted him to the high plain of continuing inward assurance, he lives radiantly, confidently, victoriously. He does not rely on another's words, but looks to the indescribable light that shines in his own soul. He has achieved an insight that neither scientific research nor philosophical argument can give him. With a confidence too deep to be disturbed by circumstance or by the vain denials of men—too strong to be destroyed by the crises of life or by the event of death—he shouts amid the noise and tumult of things, "I believe in God."

Christopher Columbus believed that the earth was round, and that on an uncharted sea he might find his way to the other side of the globe. He set out on the great adventure. Mysteries and storms engulfed him. Doubts and fears seized the heart of the men who were with him. They counseled that they turn back—as voices in the soul sometimes urge us to turn back from our quest for God and rest lazily in our unbelief. But the intrepid commander answered, "Sail on! Sail on!" Then came the day when on the horizon land appeared, and they set their feet upon a shore more beautiful and plentiful than their fondest dreams. Here is belief, and a venture, and a realization!

We who venture on our belief in God will find our fairest hopes confirmed. Belief in God, commitment to him, assurance of him and by him—this is the faith that overcomes the world. This is the key that unlocks God's treasures of grace—the conviction that undergirds all life with confidence and high expectation—the gleam that lights our pilgrim way until we come to the City of God.

NOTES